FABRIC

LAMPSHADES

-AN ILLUSTRATED GUIDE TO MAKING A VARIETY OF LAMPSHADES USING FABRIC-

BY

VARIOUS

British Library Cataloguing-in-Publication Data
A catalogue record for this book is available from the
British Library

CONTENTS

Making Lampshades

Lampshades are designed to cover light bulbs in order to diffuse the light they emit. Conical, cylindrical and other forms such as floor, desk or table-top mounted, as well as suspended lamp models are the most common, and can be made in a wide range of materials. Whilst today, lampshades serve a bigger purpose than merely dimming the glare of light bulbs - they can provide a canvas for the expression of personal, interior style; this was not always the case.

In late seventeenth century Paris, the first public lanterns, 'réverbères' made their appearance in the centre of the streets. They were oil lamps which lit the roads at night - covered with reflectors, hung above the centre of the streets. Their use soon spread to Milan, where the oil lanterns were covered by a semi-spherical reflector above the flame, which projected the light downwards, while another reflector, slightly concave and near the flame, served to direct the light latterly. This process worked reasonably well, however the introduction of 'gas light' was the innovation which necessitated shades, as opposed to reflectors. The flame, fed by gas, was intense, uniform and adjustable, white and brilliant instead of the reddish or orange of oil lamps or candles. Consequently, it had to be filtered by opal glass or light fabric shades. Lampshades were no longer used to direct the light but to attenuate it. Today, our modern electric light bulbs are no different - and the prevalence and diversification of the lampshade on every high street is a testament to its popularity.

Now, lampshades are available from almost every home furnishings store in the country. However, the only way to achieve a bespoke look, with a fabric style and colour chosen to match your room/s perfectly, is to make your own! There are three main types of lampshade, an hence construction differs substantially according to the desired outcome. But they are: 'Hard Frame', which either comes as a one piece frame or as a set of two rings (a washer top and a bottom wire ring, generally), 'Panelled Shade', which can be triangular, rectangular, square, hexagonal or bell-shaped; with vertical spokes which create the shape of pleats and panels, and 'Tailored shades', whereby the frame is measured first, and one or many different types of material are used. Hard frames are probably the simplest to make, so for the novice lampshade maker, these are the best to start with.

Making lampshades is fairly easy to do - but often hard to do neatly! Accordingly, one should leave at least an hour for the task. It does not cost a lot though, probably around twenty pounds for the kit (rings, backing material and sticky tape), plus whatever material is chosen. As a final note, fabric choice is crucial - red and yellow tones will give off a warm glow, whereas greens and blues will give off a cold light. It is also important to make sure that the fabric is not too thick or too thin, allowing the desired amount of light to escape. We hope that this book will inspire the reader to try making their own lampshades, Enjoy.

Fabric-covered Lampshades:

Methods and application. A simple lampshade — concave panels — inspection and preparation — binding materials — absence of patterns — ensuring material worked on the bias — use of pins — positioning of pins — stretching the material — covering half the frame — trimming, stitching and finishing — fitted linings. Another method — more difficult frame shape—preparation — fitting separate panels — care in stretching and pinning — sequence of pinning — even tension — stitching, finishing and decorating. A satin-covered standard lampshade — large frame — inspecting and preparing — illustration of points of instruction — different styles of treatment — separate assembly — covering the frame — fitting the lining — pinning, smoothing, trimming and stitching — importance of neatness — shaping the outer cover — marking, cutting and assembling — fitting and fastening the cover — lower panels — decoration and finishing — prowess of the home worker.

THIS chapter deals with the simple manufacture of fabric covered lampshades with sewn covers. Sewn lampshade covers are not difficult to make, if the instructions are followed carefully, and the work is done in correct sequence. Almost any fabric that does not completely block light, is suitable for use a covering material, providing it is not very openly woven, which would make it difficult to hold stitches. There are many ways of sewing fabrics covers to foundation frames. Panels may be covered separately, or several panels may be covered together, or the cover may be made in one piece for sewing to the frame. The first description is of covering a very simple frame, and the method described may be generally used for covering lampshade foundation frames of all sizes.

The lampshade foundation frame is illustrated in Fig. 11. It is a small frame for a table lamp. It has six panels which curve inwards, and it will be found that frames with concave panels are generally more suitable for covering with fabrics than frames with convex panels. The frame should be carefully checked, bent wires straightened, and rust spots removed, and the joints checked to see that they are not fractured. After checking, the frame should be bound. This may be done with bias binding in the manner previously described, or with strips of the covering material. If strips of the material are used for binding the frame they should be cut about one inch wide, and one edge of the material should be folded over and pressed, leaving the raw edge to be covered by the overlapping folded edge, but if the covering material is very thick, it would be better to use bias binding. Whatever binding is used—self or bias—the frame should be bound carefully, avoiding the formation of lumps and awkward joins, which will show under the fabric cover. To bind the type of frame illustrated, it would be best to bind all the vertical side members separately, firmly and neatly, fastening off the ends of the binding material, and finishing by binding all round the top and bottom edges. After carefully preparing the frame, it is ready for covering. Patterns are not required for the method described here.

FIG. 11. FABRIC COVERS.

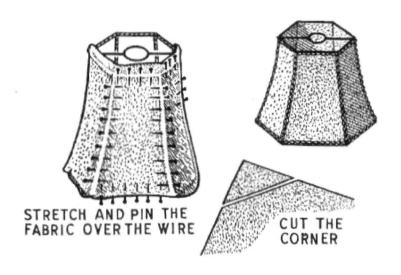

STRETCH AND PIN THE
FABRIC OVER THE WIRE

CUT THE
CORNER

There is one very important rule which must be observed when making fabric-covered lampshades. *The material must always be used on the bias,* so that stretch is even in all directions.

The illustration—Fig. 11—shows how the material is shaped over the frame. Commence by folding one corner of the material to form a triangle which can be cut off. This is to ensure that the material is used on the bias, and the trimmed corner should be parallel with the top of the frame when the cover is commenced. Using fine pins, pin the material to the top wire of the frame (as illustrated), then move to the bottom edge of the panel, and pin that also to the bound wire at the bottom of the frame. The pins in the top and bottom edges of the panels should all be vertical. Use plenty of pins to hold the material securely. After fastening the material to the top and bottom of the panel, pin one edge of the panel, fastening the pins through the material and the binding, over the wire of the frame. Pin the left edge of the panel firmly (as shown in the illustration—Fig. 11), then pull the material taut and pin through it at the right edge of the panel. All the pins at the side of the panel must be horizontal. After pinning all four sides of the panel, commence at one of the top corners, pulling the material tautly to the shape of the panel, removing one pin at a time, and replacing it after tightening the material. Work all round the panel, removing the pins, pulling tight, and replacing the pins until the material is tightly shaped over the frame panel, with no wrinkles or sagging corners; the strain should be even in all directions.

After stretching and pinning the first panel, work round to the next. Stretch and pin the top and bottom edges, and the side edge, working all round after pinning, removing pins, stretching the material, and re-pinning until the material is tightly stretched over this panel also. While shaping the material over the frame of this panel, do not allow the stretched material over the first panel to become loose. In this frame, with six small panels, it should be possible to cover one half of the frame completely with one piece of the material. When two panels are covered and pinned, the third panel may be worked, but do not take the next panel round the frame, but move back to the panel before the first panel fitted, stretching and pinning the material firmly over it.

When the three panels have been covered and the material has been evenly stretched to eliminate all wrinkles and creases, trim round the outsides of the three panels to about a quarter of an inch from the frame wire. Thread a needle with strong cotton of a suitable colour to go with the colour of the covering material, and sew the covering material to the tape-bound frame. Sew along the top edge first, turning the edge of the material under, and oversewing the folded edge. Remove the pins as the stitching progresses, but do not take out too many at a time or allow the tension on the material to be relaxed. Sew firmly along the top edge, then down the left edge of the tightened material—removing only one or two pins at a time—then along the bottom edge and up the right edge. While oversewing, trim and neaten the edges as necessary. It is not necessary to sew the material to the two upright side members of the frame in the middle of the stretched piece, and the pins holding the material to these two side-members may be removed, after all the edges have been firmly secured to the frame.

The second half of the frame should be covered in the same way as the first half, by stretching the material on *the bias* over the three remaining panels, pinning round each panel as the work progresses to remove all wrinkles and creases, and finally stitching the outside edges of the piece of material firmly and neatly to the tape-bound frame. It will be obvious from this description that the binding of the frame must be securely and tightly done in the first place. Any loose winds of binding material would not stand up to the strain of the material, and parts of the cover would sag if there were any weaknesses. When the lampshade frame has been completely covered, the inside should be inspected, and any raw edges that may show inside, should be trimmed. If the work is done carefully in the first place, and the edge of the material is trimmed as it is oversewn, there should not be any ragged edges visible in the inside of the frame.

In this method of covering a lampshade frame with fabric, a lining, if required, is easily fitted. Lining effected before the cover is fitted, can be done in exactly the same way by stretching, pinning, tightening, trimming and stitching the lining material over the tape-bound frame, but to save bulky joins at the side members, it is advisable to line only two panels at a time instead of three, arranging the edges of the lining material, so that they are not stitched to the same upright wires of the frame, as the covering material.

If the stitching is done very neatly, the lampshade may not require trimming, but in most cases fabric-covered lampshades of all sizes and types are improved by trimming. For the simple shape described above, narrow gimp or braid should be stitched over the material. First, attach the gimp or braid to upright ridges thrown into prominence by the side members, then sew strips round the top and bottom of the lampshade, covering the edges of the material.

Another method of making sewn lampshade covers is illustrated in Fig. 12. The frame shown is a medium-large one, suitable for a large table lampshade or a small standard shade. The foundation frame is separated into eight panels which have concave and convex curves. The frame is fitted with a 'duplex' ring for attachment to an adjustable gate-leg gimbal fitting. In making the sewn cover, each panel division is treated separately.

The first thing to do is to inspect the frame and bind all the wires with bias binding or strips of the material which is to be used for making the cover. The binding material should be firmly bound round the wire, and firmly fastened off to take the strain of the tight cover. When the frame has been made, covering should commence. Remember the most important rule of covering with fabrics is to *always* work the material on the bias so that the stretch is even. Fold one corner of the material over, as previously explained and illustrated, cut the corner off, and place the material over one of the panels with the cut corner level with the top of the frame. Pin through the top edge of the material to secure it to the bound wire at the top of the foundation frame, with the pins placed vertically. Use plenty of pins to ensure holding the material firmly. Up to this point, the instructions have been almost the same as those given for making the first fabric-covered lampshade, but from here they differ, as the shade previously described had concave panels only.

FIG. 12. COVERING SHAPED PANELS.

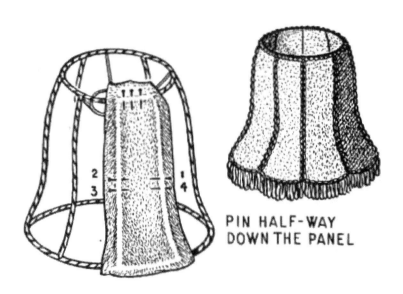

PIN HALF-WAY
DOWN THE PANEL

When the top of the material is firmly affixed to the top of the frame, pin at the bottom of the panel, but do *not* pull the material too tightly. Merely insert a pin to fasten the centre of the material to the middle of the base panel wire as a guide. It will be seen from the shape of the foundation frame that if the bottom edge of the material is pinned firmly, and the material is stretched, it will leave a gap between the foundation frame and fabric at the upper part of the panel, which is concave. To fit the covering fabric over the curved panel, work down both sides of the panel wires at the same time. Use plenty of pins and insert them horizontally through the material and the frame binding. Place a pin through one edge of the panel covering, then pull the material tight, and insert a pin in the other edge of the panel opposite the first pin. Pin again under the *second* pin inserted, then stretch the material from the other side of the panel and insert the fourth pin (the pins are numbered in the illustration—Fig. 12—to clarify this explanation). The fifth pin should be inserted under the fourth pin. Continue working in this way, inserting two pins at each side of the panel, and pulling the material tight as the pinning is done, to a point halfway down the panel, where the concave curve becomes convex. When pinning the top half of the panel, move the bottom pin as necessary, merely using it as a guide to the centre of the panel covering. After passing the forward curve, the bottom edge of the panel covering should be firmly pinned to the binding at the bottom of the frame. Insert the first pin at the bottom, in the middle, then work from this pin outwards to the panel edges, inserting a pin alternately each side of the first pin, pulling the material taut all the while. When the bottom is firmly secured, pin the bottom half of the edges of the covering to the wire covered frames at the sides of the panel. Care should be taken at every stage, to ensure that the tension of the material is even in all directions.

Go all round the panel, removing a pin at a time and pulling the material tight, to smooth out all wrinkles and creases. When the panel is smooth and tight, trim the material to a quarter of an inch of the wires, and commence stitching. Start at the top left corner and use strong cotton of the same colour as the covering material. Turn the edge of the material under and oversew the fold to the frame binding. Stitch all round the edge of the panel, neatly and firmly, removing one or two pins at a time, and maintaining an even tension of the covering fabric. After working all round the panel, fasten off firmly and neaten all raw edges inside the lampshade. When experience is gained with practise, it will be found possible to neaten the edges as the panel is sewn in place.

The remaining seven panels are covered in the same way as the first, taking care to work the material on the bias and maintaining even tension of the panels. When the cover is finished, it should be decorated with braid, gimp or silk cord. For a shade of the size and shape of the one described, a wide gimp would be suitable to cover the joins between the panels, and to edge the frame. A fringe could be attached, if required.

The third fabric-covered lampshade described is rather more difficult to make, than the two previously mentioned. The frame is illustrated in Fig. 13. It is a large frame for a standard lampshade, and is fitted with a 'duplex' ring. It is a fairly simple shape to cover, but to illustrate another method of fitting fabric covers, it is described as being covered with white satin. The top edge is trimmed with silver-coloured braid, the two bottom edges are also trimmed with silver braid, and the bottom edge will have a deep fringe of silvery silk cord, but the upright seams of the body of the cover are not to be covered with braid or gimp. Obviously, such a lampshade of this description would only be suitable for use with a complementary furnishing scheme, and the purpose of describing this lampshade, is to illustrate some points of instruction for making all types of fabric-covered shades—for this purpose, the quality of the material, colouring, shape and style of trimming could be changed to suit a particular requirement. Two different styles of treatment are described in making the sewn cover. The top part of the covering is marked to shape over the foundation frame, but it is not stitched direct to the frame. It is assembled separately and fastened to the frame as one piece. The panels in the lower half of the lampshade are fitted and attached directly to the frame.

The lampshade is lined, and, for use with satin, a fine texture such as Lawn, is suitable.

FIG. 13. A TAILORED COVER.

The foundation frame should be very carefully checked for inaccuracies and faults, and although care in checking is necessary as a preliminary to covering lampshades with any type of material, extra care should be taken when using expensive covering materials. After checking and rectifying any faults, the frame should be carefully bound with bias binding of a suitable colour, or with strips of the lining material. Use of the lining material is preferable to the covering material. Bind the frame carefully and firmly. Cover all the upright wires first, then bind the three wires running round the frame. The foundation of binding must be attached very firmly and ends should be fastened off securely.

When the preparation has been satisfactorily completed, the work of covering the frame should commence. First, the lining is attached. A corner of the lining material should be cut (as previously described), to ensure that the material is attached on the bias. The treatment of the lining is as previously described. The material should be carefully fitted over each panel, from the *inside* of the frame, and secured with pins. The material should be kept very tight, by working round each panel, removing pins and stretching, to pull out any wrinkles or creases, before replacing the pins. The top panels should be lined first, and the panels at the bottom of the frame lined last. Two or more panels may be lined together, according to the size of the lining material. Great care should be taken in trimming, turning and sewing the edges of the lining material to the foundation frame. Although it is unlikely that much of the work will be visible when the lampshade is in use, neatness in attaching the lining is essential, especially if the lampshade is being made for sale. Trim and fold the edges of the lining material, removing one or two pins at a time, and sewing with fine neat stitches. The edges of the material should be arranged to come halfway over the supporting wires. The lower panels of the frame will be found quite easy to line separately, using small pieces of material. After lining has been completed, trim any raw edges of the material inside the lining (that is from the outside of the frame).

When the lining has been satisfactorily fitted, the main

cover may be made. Each panel should be fitted separately over the frame. Commence with any of the panels. Cut a triangular corner of the satin to work the material on the bias, pin through the top edge of the material to the top wire of the frame, using *very* fine pins with the right side of the material outside. Pin the bottom edge next, keeping the material smooth. Pin the edges of the panel, then work carefully round it, moving pins and stretching the material, until the panel is tightly and smoothly covered. Arrange the pins as shown in the illustration, so that the material may be marked where it covers the wire. The outline of the panel should be marked on the material and this is best done with chalk which can be brushed off when the cover has been stitched. Mark all round the panel over the middle of the bound wires. Remove all the pins and trim the material to the panel shape at the edges, allowing an extra one quarter to three-eighths of an inch for turning. The top and bottom need not be trimmed at this stage. As the panels are stretched, marked and cut, they should be kept in the order of making so that, when fastened together, each panel covering is stretched over the actual panel to which it was fitted. This is important because there may be some differences in the sizes of the panels. After cutting all the eight panels of the top of the cover, they may be fastened together. Fig. 14 illustrates how the panels are joined on the wrong side of the material. Accuracy in stitching is essential and is best done on a sewing machine. Stitch the eight panels together, press and neaten the seams and fasten off firmly.

After assembling the top of the cover, it should be fitted over the lined frame. This should be done carefully, ensuring that the seams fit exactly over the upright side-members. Place the cover over the frame as far as it will go, then work round, gently pulling each panel down until the cover is smooth and unwrinkled. Use fine pins to keep the bottom edge of the cover in place, then pin round the top edge through the frame binding. Keep working round the lampshade removing one pin at a time and stretching the cover smoothly over the frame. If the panels were sewn together properly, there should be no wrinkles across the material. Care should be taken when fitting the cover not to ruck any of the pressed seams where they cover the frame wires. When you are fully satisfied that the cover is perfectly fitted, commence stitching the top edge of the satin to the frame binding. Trim and fold the material. Stitch neatly and firmly, removing one or two pins at a time and keeping the tension on the material. Stitch all round the top of the cover, then sew the bottom of the cover to the binding, over the uppermost wire of the lower panels. Keep the material smooth and taut while sewing, and fasten off firmly.

When the top part of the cover has been fitted and sewn, the small lower panels should be covered. These small panels may be covered singly with pieces of satin left over from the main cover. Work one small panel at a time, making certain that the material is used on the bias. Pin along the top edge first, then stretch the material and pin the bottom edge, pinning the sides of the panel last. Work round the panel several times, moving the pins and tightening the material. Trim the edges of the panel with a sharp pair of scissors and stitch the edges of the material to the frame, removing one or two pins at a time, and trimming and folding the edge under, as the sewing progresses. Cover all the eight lower panels. After the cover has been completed, the braid should be attached.

FIG. 14. JOINING THE PANELS.

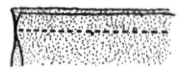

STITCH THROUGH
THE WRONG SIDE

Stitch the silver braid to the top of the lampshade first, covering the edges of lining and satin with the braid. Fasten the ends of the braid neatly. Then affix braid to each upright edge dividing the panels. Fasten the ends neatly. Stitch braid round the top edge of the lower panels covering the joins of the material. Attach the fringe next, to the bottom edge of the lampshade, and finish by sewing braid over the top of the fringe.

The manufacture of these 'luxury' lampshades is not beyond the capability of the home worker, providing that the work is done in sequence and each stage of the work is carried out carefully. It is repeated that lampshades of the type described above would be suitable only for use amid certain surroundings, but the knowledge presented in the instructions is generally useful to the lampshade maker for making all classes of sewn fabric covers. There is unlimited scope in making large lampshades of this type to order, and it can be a very profitable pastime.

SECTIONAL FABRIC SHADES

[PHOTOGRAPH 1A]

THIS method of covering lampshades is used for any convex or unusual shape, where the method described in Chapter 12 would be impracticable. Almost any soft fabric can be used, but the easiest to manipulate are silk, satin, crepe, brocade, cotton and rayon. All materials should be cut on the straight.

Bedhead shades usually need to have each panel covered separately and the covering of one of these is described below.

Method of Making

1. Tape the frame and dye the taped frame to the colour of the material.

2. Pin a piece of material across the centre panel, remembering that if there is a pattern on the material it must be fixed in the centre of the panel. Stretch and pull the material pinning it to the section of the frame until it is quite taut and free from creases (Fig. 38).

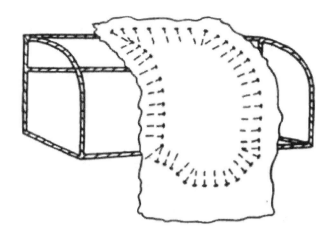

FIG. 38 (*above*). Single section of material pinned to centre section of bedhead frame

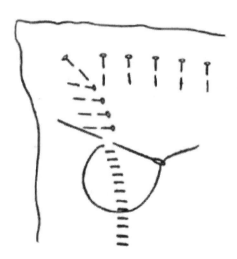

FIG. 39. Attaching material with small oversewing stitches

3. Stitch this section firmly to the frame with close oversewing stitches, removing the pins as the stitching progresses (Fig. 39).

4. Turn the surplus material over on to the right side of the shade and lash it down over the first row of stitching. Cut away the surplus material close to these lashing stitches (Fig. 40).

5. Cover the remainder of the shade in similar fashion, covering one section at a time and remembering that the back section of a bedhead shade should be double, and contain a piece of asbestos to protect the bed from the heat.

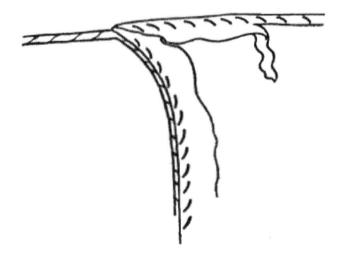

FIG. 40. Material lashed and being trimmed back

6. Hide the raw edges with trimming, covering the vertical struts first, and then the horizontal joins and edges.

Frames of unusual shapes, but with all the sections of the same shape, can have each section covered separately, or two or even three sections covered with one piece of material, according to the shape of the frame and the appearance required of the finished shade.

Method of Making

1. Tape the frame and dye it to the required colour.
2. Decide how many sections are to be covered at once.
3. Cut sufficient pieces of material to cover all the sections, allowing at least 1 in. to spare all round each piece.

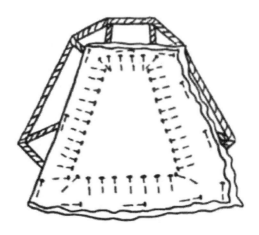

FIG. 41. Double material pinned to one section of the frame

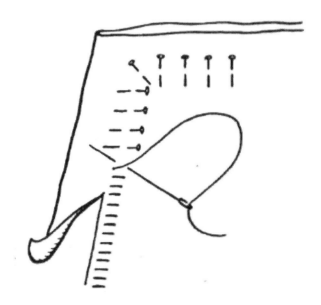

FIG. 42. Double material stitched to one strut and the surplus trimmed close to the stitching

4. Take two pieces of material, right sides together, and pin them together round the edges.
5. Pin these two pieces of material over the section to be covered first. Pull them taut and adjust the pins until there are no creases (Fig. 41).

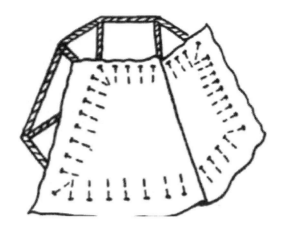

FIG. 43. Material opened out and pinned over two sections

6. Stitch both pieces to one vertical strut using small neat oversewing stitches (Fig. 42).

7. Trim the surplus material very close to the stitching (Fig. 42).

8. Remove all the pins and open out the two pieces of material. Pin them down over two sections making sure they are both taut and free from creases (Fig. 43).

9. Take a third piece of material and place it right side down over the left-hand section and pin it over the material already pinned in place on the left-hand strut. The pins in this third piece of material should go right into the underpiece and through the tape of the frame.

10. When it is firmly in place, remove the lower layer of pins,

and stitch both pieces of material into place on the left-hand strut.

11. Trim off any surplus material close to the stitching.

12. Continue covering the sections in this manner until the last piece is attached. Then pin it carefully over the first piece which is still pinned on to its right-hand strut.

13. Unpin and lift this last piece of material and fold it under along the pin marks just made.

14. Stitch the first piece to its right-hand strut, and trim the raw edge down to the stitching.

15. Pin the folded edge carefully over the first section and stitch it firmly to the material and the strut.

16. Trim away the surplus material from inside this last turning.

17. Pull and pin the material into place right over the top and bottom of the frame and then stitch it to the frame with small oversewing stitches.

18. Turn the surplus material over to the front of the shade and lash it down with large stitches. Trim off any surplus material close to these lashing stitches.

19. Cover the top and bottom of the shade with trimming.

A BOWED EMPIRE SHADE
WITH A BALLOON LINING

[PHOTOGRAPHS 3C, 4A, 4D]

THIS IS a particularly attractive and expensive looking shade for a table-lamp, a hanging light, or a floor standard. Like the sectional shades described in the previous chapter, it is made from material cut on the straight. Satin, silk or crepe are the most usual materials for this type of shade. Taffeta will not pull sufficiently, and fabrics such as nylon are apt to slacken and crinkle if they get into a damp atmosphere. The lining should be made of a very light colour. White crepe is excellent for this purpose. The frame required is known as a bowed Empire.

Method of Making

1. Tape the frame. There is no need to dye the tapes as the frame will be completely lined and all the taping hidden.

2. Cut two pieces of material, one for the lining and one for the outer cover. The amount of material required can be calculated as follows:

29

width = circumference of bottom ring plus at least 4 in.

depth = length of a bowed strut plus at least 2 in.

3. First make the lining. Fold the material in two with the right side out, and pin it together all round the edges.

4. Lay this double material over half the frame and pin it to the frame at the four 'corners' of the half frame.

This is a temporary attachment of the material to the frame and it is probable that the position of these pins will need to be adjusted several times before the final position is definitely fixed.

5. Pulling the material taut across the waist of the shade, pin it at frequent intervals to the two side struts. Adjust the position of the pins until there are no creases down the struts.

6. Again pulling the material, but this time gently over the top ring, pin the material in position there.

7. Finally, pull tightly over the bottom ring, and pin the material to it (Fig. 44).

It cannot be stressed too often that much care and patience must be exercised in this fixing of the material to the frame, and in its final position there should be no creases whatever on either side of the double piece of material.

8. Now take a needle and thread and run a line of tacking

stitches through the double material outside the struts, but as close to them as possible. These stitches must not attach the material to the frame at any point.

9. Now remove the pins which hold the material to the frame, and take off the double piece of material which is still held in shape by the pins round the edge and the tacking stitches. It will be noticed that at the top, the stitching curves inwards (Fig. 45).

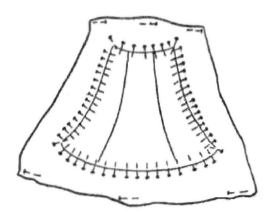

FIG. 44. Double material stretched and pinned across half the frame

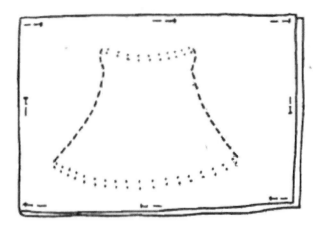

FIG. 45. Material removed from the frame and showing pin marks and tacking

10. Make a french seam down each side. The first row of stitching must come exactly over the tacking stitches, and should continue beyond them for a short distance both at top and bottom. Then cut away the surplus material at the sides, turn the material, and make a small neat french seam.

11. Make the outer cover in exactly the same way (paras. 3–10).

12. Now take the lining, wrong side out, and place it inside the frame. The original pin marks should show quite clearly, and the lining should be pinned first to the bottom ring through those marks, making sure that the french seams are hidden behind the struts.

13. Next fix the lining over the top ring. First, pin the seams at the top only, so that they lie behind the struts. Then pull and adjust the material, pinning it to the top ring until there are no creases anywhere, and cutting carefully to allow the material to be pinned round the fitment. The pins will probably need to be adjusted several times both on the top and bottom rings before a final position is fixed.

14. Stitch the lining to the tape of both rings with a very close oversewing stitch. The lining should be carried right over the rings and stitched on the outside of the frame (Fig. 46).

15. Cut away the surplus material, close to the stitching (Fig. 46).

16. Now take the outer cover, right side out, and slip it over the lined frame. Make sure that the french seams lie over the same strut as the french seams of the lining.

FIG. 46. *Top left.* Balloon lining stitched into the frame and being trimmed back to the stitching

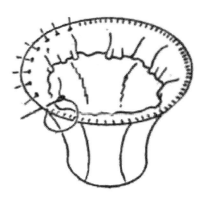

FIG. 47. *Above.* Outer cover being stitched over the lining

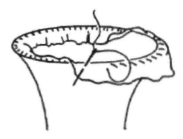

FIG. 48. Surplus material of outer cover folded back and lashed down

17. Pin the outer cover to the top and bottom rings over the lining, pulling and adjusting the material as before. The seams must lie absolutely straight over the struts or they will show too much when the lamp is lighted.

18. Stitch the outer cover to both top and bottom rings. The cover should be carried over the lining and the rings, and stitched so as to completely cover the stitching of the lining (Fig. 47).

19. Fold the surplus material back over the stitching and lash it down with long stitches, at the front of the rings (Fig. 48). Then cut off any surplus.

20. Attach trimmings as required.

A LACE OR NET OVER SATIN SHADE

[PHOTOGRAPHS 3A AND 4C]

VERY attractive shades can be made with the use of transparent or semi-transparent materials such as lace, net, organdie, etc., fixed to the frame immediately over a silk or satin fabric. The shiny surface of the silk or satin gives 'body' to the lace which, while looking attractive in the daytime, becomes doubly so when lighted. Different combinations of colour can be used with good effect. Coffee-coloured lace or net over pink, peach or maize coloured satin fixed to a petal shaped frame (Fig. 2*e*) makes a particularly attractive shade, and the making of it is described below.

The amount of material required is calculated as follows:

It is cut on the STRAIGHT.

Width: The material when doubled must go round the widest part of half the frame, plus 2 or 3 in. for 'play'.

Depth: The material must cover the longest part of the frame i.e. from the top to the bottom of a petal, allowing for the curve of the struts, plus 2 or 3 in. for 'play'.

Method of Making

1. Place the lace over the satin, and fold both in two with the right sides out. Pin the pieces carefully together round the edges so that there are no creases anywhere.

2. Fix the four thicknesses to the frame and make the cover in exactly the same way as for a bowed Empire shade (see Chapter 12, paras. 4–10).

3. Slip the double material over the outside of the frame, so that the seams lie exactly over the struts. Otherwise they will show when the lamp is lighted.

4. Pin the double material over the petals at the top and bottom of the frame, pulling and pinning it until there are no creases in either the satin or the net. It will probably be found that the pins need to be adjusted several times before a final taut position is fixed.

5. Stitch both materials to the frame at once, stitching to the top of the frame first, and the bottom last. The materials should be pulled right over the frame and attached with close oversewing stitches as far inside the frame as possible. It will probably be found necessary to snip the material to ease it into the bottom of the petals. Great care must be taken not to cut too far, or the material will fray when pulled and eventually tear away.

6. Turn the surplus material back to the outside of the frame and lash it down on the outside of both the top

and bottom of the petals, using large stitches which will be covered by the trimming.

7. Cut away the surplus material close to the lashing stitches.

8. Attach trimming to both the top and bottom of the frame, either by stitching, or the use of an adhesive. When an adhesive is used, it is always advisable to try attaching a small piece of trimming to a spare piece of material first, to ensure that the adhesive does not leave any marks on either material or trimming.

A FRENCH SHADE

FRENCH shades are usually made of taffeta or satin and are, as a rule, heavily trimmed, either with lace or ruched velvet, or rows of piping cord under satin, with ruched satin or velvet between the rows of piping. The making of a simple lace-trimmed French shade is described below.

The frame required is known as a French frame. It is similar to a straight Empire, with a collar attached to the top ring (Fig. 2*d*, page 11).

The method of making is as follows:

1. Tape the frame.
2. Line the frame, either with a balloon lining (see Chapter 12, page 72), or with a pleated lining. (See Chapter 15, page 84.)
3. Trim the bottom edge of the lining with a plain ruching.
4. (*a*) Cut a length of material equal to 6 times the diameter of the bottom ring. The depth of the material is calculated as follows:

The length of the struts from the bottom of the collar, plus 1/4 of this length, plus 1 in. for turnings, e.g. with a shade whose struts measure 7 in., the material will be cut 7 in. plus 1 3/4 in. plus 1 in.= 9 3/4 in. deep.

(*b*) Cut also a piece of material equal in length to 6 times the diameter of the bottom ring and in depth equal to 1/4 of the length of the struts, plus 1 1/2 in.

(*c*) Cut also a piece of stiffened book muslin equal in length to 6 times the diameter of the bottom ring, and in depth equal to 1/4 of the length of the struts plus 1/2 in.

(*d*) Cut also a piece of material equal in length to the circumference of the collar and as deep as the collar plus 1 in. for turnings.

5. Join together the two pieces of material 4(*a*) and 4(*b*) along the long cut edges, so that when the seam is finished and the smaller piece turned over on to the larger, the right sides of both pieces of material are facing upwards.
6. Place the length of stiffened muslin between the two pieces of material, turn the top edging of the narrower piece over the muslin and stitch it into place. This stiffened width forms the bottom of the shade.
7. Take a piece of lace a fraction wider than the muslin and stich it over the stiffened portion.
8. Join the two ends of the material together with a narrow french seam, or a flat seam.
9. Gather or pleat the top edge of the material and stitch it

firmly to the bottom of the collar (Fig. 49).

10. Stitch the piece of material cut for the collar over this to hide the raw edges and finish it off tightly at the top of the frame.

FIG. 49. French Shade, gathered and stitched to the bottom of the collar

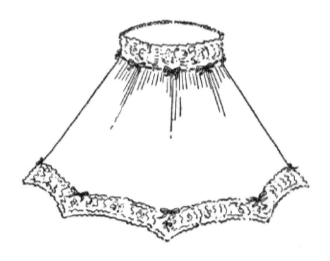

FIG. 50. French Shade with the collar and trimming added

11. Trim around the collar with a width of lace.
12. Attach the shade to the bottom of each strut in equal flutes. Trim with small ribbon bows over each of these points to hide any stitching and attach matching bows around the collar (Fig. 50).

PLEATED AND SWATHED SILK SHADES

[PHOTOGRAPHS 7 AND 8]

PLEATED silk shades can be made in three ways, all of them simple, and giving very pleasing results. The materials most often used are silk, rayon, chiffon, georgette, nylon, etc. It is essential that a frame with fixed struts should be used, and generally they are straight sided frames. A pleasing effect can, however, be obtained by lining a bowed Empire frame with a balloon lining and then making a straight pleated cover outside. In the cavity thus made it is possible to fix artificial flowers or cut-out designs which only show when the lamp is lighted.

The shades described below are all made on straight Empire frames. They are unlined and are made of silk or rayon. If materials such as chiffon or georgette are used, a balloon lining should be put in.

Method of Making, No. 1

1. Tape the frame, and dye it to the colour of the material being used.

2. Take a piece of material cut on the straight, and equal in

length to the circumference of the bottom of the frame, and about 1 in. wider than the depth of the frame.

3. With the wrong side of the material outwards and hanging below the frame, pin one long edge to the bottom ring, starting at a strut. The material must be very tightly pulled round the frame (Fig. 51).

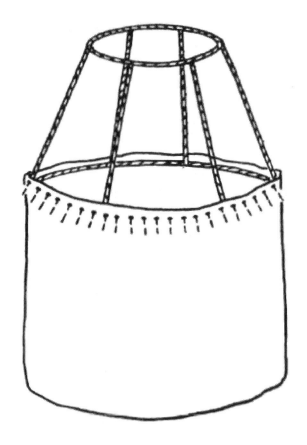

FIG. 51. Pleated Shade. Method 1. Material pinned tightly

to bottom ring

4. With close oversewing stitches, attach the material to the bottom of the frame. Where the stitching finishes and the material overlaps, make a neat flat seam right down the material. Trim the raw edges against the bottom of the frame.

5. Count the number of struts and divide the material equally into a similar number of parts. Mark each division with a pin or tailors' chalk.

6. Turn the material up and attach it to the top of each strut at the corresponding pin mark.

FIG. 52. Pleated Shade. Method 1. Material pleated and pinned to top ring

7. Make even pleats in the material between the struts at the top of the frame, and pin each pleat to the top ring (Fig. 52).

8. Stitch the pleated material to the top ring with close oversewing stitches.

9. Turn the surplus material over to the outside of the frame and lash it down with long stitches. Trim the material down to these lashing stitches.

10. Cover the top and bottom of the frame with trimming.

This method can be used to make a lining for French and other shades. The only variation in the method is that the material is pinned to the bottom of the frame with the RIGHT side outwards, and, after stitching, is turned up inside the frame and pinned over the top ring.

Method of Making, No. 2

1. Tape the frame and dye it to the colour of the material being used.

2. Take a piece of material cut on the straight, equal in length to 3 times the circumference of the top ring, and about 2 in. wider than the depth of the frame.

3. Fold one long edge of the material into 1/2-in. pleats and pin each pleat securely to the top ring, starting with the short edge of the material lying down a strut. The last piece should just overlap this to hide the raw edge.

4. Taper the pleats from the top of the frame to the bottom

and pin them in place on the bottom ring.

5. Stitch the material to the top and bottom rings of the frame with close oversewing stitches. Turn the surplus material over to the outside of the shade and lash it down with large stitches. Trim off any surplus material close to the lashing stitches.

6. Attach trimming to the top and bottom of the shade.

Method of Making, No. 3

This is simply binding round and round the frame with ribbon, slightly overlapping it round the bottom of the frame, making wider overlaps round the narrower top ring, and causing a pleated effect.

1-in. wide ribbon is generally used. The amount required can be calculated by measuring the depth of the shade, multiplying it by 2, and then multiplying the result by the length of the circumference of the bottom ring in inches. It is wise to add at least 1/2 yard for overlapping.

1. Tape the frame.

2. Stitch one end of the ribbon to the inside of the bottom ring, against a strut.

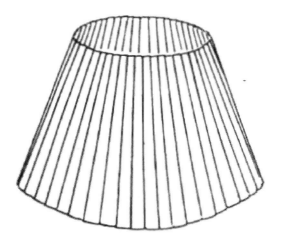

FIG. 53. Pleated Shade. Method 3. Ribbon wound round the frame

3. Carry the ribbon over the top ring and down under the bottom ring. Overlap the first piece of ribbon very slightly and carry the ribbon to the top again. Here it must be well overlapped.

   Continue in this way all round the frame, making sure that the edge of the ribbon is straight at, and parallel to, each strut (Fig. 53). If it is not, then the overlapping at the top ring is inaccurate, and must be adjusted, or the pleating will be crooked.

4. When the last overlap has been made, fasten off the ribbon by turning under the raw edge and stitching it

neatly against the first piece.

If the beginning and ending is neatly done, there is no need for any trimming, unless it is particularly desired.

SWATHED SHADES
[PHOTOGRAPH 7]

These are made in a similar way to Method No. 2 above, but the first pleat is attached to the bottom of one strut, carried round the frame and attached to the top of the second or third strut round, depending on the angle of the swathe required and the number of struts on the frame. The following pleats are pinned successively to the bottom ring and overlapped to the top ring.

The swathed shade described below is made of satin, with a crepe balloon lining, on a bowed Empire frame.

The amount of material required can be calculated as follows:

The material is cut on the STRAIGHT.

Length: Must be equal to three times the circumference of the bottom ring.

Depth: The distance from the bottom of one strut round to the top of the second or third strut (according to the angle of the swathe required), plus about 4 in.

Method of Making

1. Tape the frame.

2. Make a balloon lining (see Chapter 12, paras. 2–10), but do not fix it to the frame until the swathing has been attached.

3. Take one piece of satin and fold under 1/2 in. along the short side. Pin the bottom edge of the short side to the bottom of a strut leaving about 3/4 in. of material below the frame. Carry the short edge tautly round the frame and pin it to the top of the second or third strut. Note that there is about 3 in. of surplus material above the top of the frame (Fig. 54).

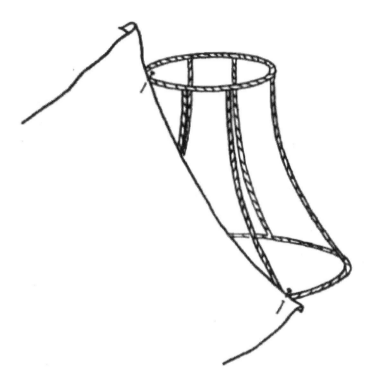

FIG. 54. Swathed Shade. First fold pinned around the frame

4. Make sufficient 1/2-in. pleats in the bottom of the material to carry it round to the next strut, and pin each to the bottom of the frame.

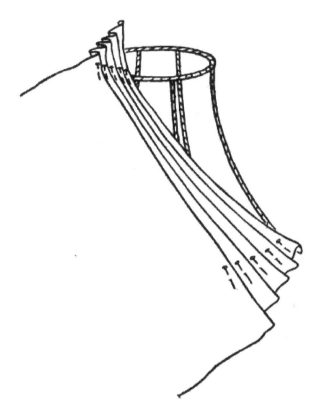

FIG. 55. Swathed Shade. Pleating carried round the frame. Note how the surplus material decreases at the top

5. Carry these pleats to the top of the frame, overlapping them so that the same number of pleats lies between a pair of struts at both the top and bottom of the frame (Fig. 55).

6. It will be noticed that the surplus material at the top of the frame gradually becomes shorter as the number of

pleats increases. When it has decreased to about 3/4 in., cut the material off parallel to the last pleat, leaving 1 in. of material from the edge of the last fold.

7. Pin a new pleat over this cut edge, allowing 3/4 in. of material to fall below the bottom of the frame as in the case of the first pleat made, and repeat the pleating as described above until the shade is completely covered. When the last pleat has been made, cut off the material about 1 in. from the last fold, take out the pins holding the first pleat, and re-pin it over the last cut edge.

8. Hold the shade over a light and adjust any pleats which do not appear to be even.

9. Stitch the pleats to the top and bottom of the frame with close oversewing stitches, carrying the material as far over the frame as possible before stitching (Fig. 47). Then cut off any surplus material close to the stitching.

10. Now put in the balloon lining (see Chapter 12, paragraphs 12–14) carrying the edges right over the top and bottom rings and stitch them down over the pleating. Cut the surplus lining material back to the stitching.

11. Attach trimming to the top and bottom of the shade.

Printed in Great Britain
by Amazon